Snapshots in Time

Robyn Lindsey

ISBN: **989541614**
ISBN-13: **978-0989541619**

DEDICATION

This book is dedicated to all the loves in my life. Past, present, and future.
My amazing sons, my love, Aaron, friends and family who have been in my
life, who have encouraged me, even those who have angered me. Each and
every relationship I have had has inspired me to write poetry. I am ever so
thankful.

CONTENTS

ACKNOWLEDGMENTS

I have been a reader of poetry my entire life. Robert Frost, Shel Silverstein, Nikki Giovanni, Marge Piercy, Adrienne Rich, Allen Ginsberg, Anne Sexton, Mr. Henson (my highschool friend's dad who wrote amazing poetry). I thank all of these and more for their influence on my life.

1. THE BEGINNING

I had a tumultuous childhood. My parents divorced soon after I was born, then when I was either 4 or 5, we moved from Utah to South Texas. We moved to live with my grandparents, as my mother had been diagnosed with Multiple Sclerosis. To this day, I can not imagine having to make that type of decision. To pick up and move your entire life about 20 steps backwards. To leave your two oldest (adult) children and take your three youngest ones and show up at your parent's doorstep.

I had seen my grandparents a couple times prior to our move. They had traveled to see us in their motor home. I knew that my grandmother did NOT want to be called "Grandma" as she felt that made her sound too old. She wanted to be called "Nanaw". I slipped and called her Grandma when we arrived. She didn't make a big deal about it, but I remember being seriously frightened of her.

I grew to know that she was kinder than she was scary, but it was often a very delicate balance. Let me be clear about something before assumptions are made. I think my grandparents were amazing people. They took their ill daughter in, along with 3 grandchildren aged 5, 7, and 9. They were ready to retire and travel and they lost that.

I think they were strict, and reactive, but I do not fault them for that. Their lives took a turn that no one could have predicted. I will tell you also that I don't recall all that was told to me about my grandparents prior to moving in with them, but I never quite lost the fear.

Possibly due to that fear, I became a quiet child who was in my head a lot. As a teen, when hormones threatened to take over my being, I began writing poetry. It was my outlet, and I believed that throughout my life, poetry has saved me more than once.

I have continued to write poetry to this day, with times of no writing interspersed throughout. I have found that I reach out to poetry when I need it, and push it aside when all is well. It just is the relationship that we have, and it works.

I will put my poetry throughout this book. Some will speak to you in ways you had not imagined, as poetry often has the tendency to do.

Much of my poetry is reactionary to actions of others, my way of staying sane in situations that threaten my sanity. Much of it allowed me to have a voice where I felt I had none.

I welcome you to dive in and devour the entire book, or take small nibbles. When you find something that speaks to you, share with someone else. Thank you so much for being here.

2 THE POETRY

Shattered Spirit

I never loved you.

You were opposition

to everything I believed in.

Yet, there was an attraction.

Was there a lesson to be learned?

Or was fate just being cruel?

You changed me,

everything I believed in.

My inhibitions were replaced

with your assuredness.

You picked up my life and

shattered my glass walls.

Then, once more, I was left all alone

Trying to pick up the pieces,

and mend the shattered spirit.

Scars

The implications of relationships

are so messy.

Each and every time we embark

on a new relationship, we leave imprints

whether we mean to or not.

We leave impressions on hearts.

Some of those imprints will be filled in

by others.

But some will be so deep

that they will only scar.

Inner Strength

I feel like

I am constantly

swimming upstream.

At every turn

I am faced with obstacles.

There are times

that I think of

turning back,

of giving up.

But instead, I hold

my head high

and forge onward.

Love Without Bounds

How many loves

can one person have?

Is there a set number?

I love so many,

I have loved so many.

I love my children,

each in their own way.

My friends, for so many reasons.

My cheerleaders

My confidantes

My secret crushes

I love so fully, and without apology.

A difference of opinion

You use your bible as a shield

to keep heathens like me at bay.

Somehow I penetrated your defenses.

That confuses you, makes you frightened.

You don't know whether to embrace me,

shove me away,

or anoint me with holy water.

The depths of your being knows

that I mean you no harm.

More confusion—

aren't people like me out to hurt you—

or at least on a mission to change your beliefs?

Afraid of my attack, you don't ask.

You know that I don't think the same as you.

I look at people in a way different from you.

I know you are who you are.

I know that you have your reasons just as I have mine.

I respect your beliefs.

In a perfect world you would treat me with the same respect.

For Maria, on her 34th Birthday

I think about how it seems

That our lives parallel

How often we must be

thinking the same thing,

or doing the same thing.

and I think...

maybe it's not just us.

maybe it's every woman—

always the same pursuits—

Love, family, friends, a career

and with each endeavor,

we hope beyond all other hope

to not have to sell our soul

like we've been asked to do

so many times before.

We've sold our souls

for men, for jobs, for our children

and each time that our soul

is the price, things end badly.

Perhaps

all of those times only strengthen us—

and get us to the point

where we know exactly what we want

because we now know everything that we

don't want,

everything that we will no longer do.

And once we meet people worthy of us,

who don't demand a sacrifice—

who will accept who we are,

only then can our fractured soul

fully repair.

Five Hours

A five hour drive.

That's all it takes for me to end up

in a place where I feel completely foreign.

I lived here a long time

but now I wonder did I ever belong?

This place makes my skin crawl,

robs me of my peace,

takes away my energy.

I wonder

was this drive necessary?

Was it meant to be the catalyst to healing?

I came.

Now I will sit silently in this space

and reclaim me.

Evolution

Love morphs into hate

passion into ambivalence

friendship into romance.

Every phase of life is about evolution.

Each time we settle in, the rules change.

In order to survive, we must also morph.

If we are unbending,

if we make ourselves unmalleable—

out of fear

or....

well, almost always out of fear,

we will not survive,

at least not whole.

We will fragment.

Dad

Dad.

That word has as many meanings

as there are people in this world.

My father, frail and in his twilight years.

He is absent, as he has been my whole life.

He has not held me as I've cried.

He has never doled out any advice,

paid for my education,

taught me how to drive,

or scared the hell out of prospective dates.

He is a man I do not know.

I call him every few years and he never calls me.

I love him for reasons

I will never be able to explain.

I do not love him for all that he's done.

I love that he helped give me life.

I believe that he even loves me.

And there must be reasons for his absence.

I used to hate his lack of concern.

But with age comes wisdom.

Perhaps he never knew how to be what I needed.

Perhaps he thought I was better off without him.

So, to my frail dad in his twilight years, I say...

Dad,

I love you.

I love the person that I have become

and I would never change a thing.

So thank you for all you never did.

I have no regrets and hope that life

as you lived it was everything

you had wished for.

** Note: I wrote this when I was in my early 30's. Dad and I reconnected and had an amazing relationship up until his death in 2010. He would have fully understood this poem, though it would have made him sad.

Fire

Burning.

A huge firestorm,

a veritable inferno

of passion,

longing,

pure need.

Afterwards, shell shocked,

we can look back and surmise

the damage done.

The fire burns red hot

and grows.

Only after all oxygen is consumed

does it die down.

Who is left when it is done?

Are either left unharmed?

Can wounds heal?

And if so, what is the bandage?

Small Minds

He called me 'liberal girl'

he spat the words at me

as if they were poison.

I knew he meant to hurt

but the words didn't sting.

I wondered if it's how

black people feel

when called 'niggers'.

The label only shows the

closed minded ignorance

of those doing the labeling.

It doesn't hurt because

those speaking aren't

worth being hurt by.

Madness

I am a witness to madness every day.

We all have ways of self-torture.

Some pull you in

while pushing away at the same time.

Some move at you like a freight train

and they move so fast you can't jump away

from their destruction.

Others close themselves off completely

and refuse to let you in no matter

how hard you try.

Leadership

Your world is all smoke and mirrors

You know how to succeed,

your ideas appear amazing

and people flock to them

but the newness wears off

you prove that it was all a hoax

all lies to draw people in

and make a buck off of them.

I watch you and I learn.

I learn how not to do it,

I learn the importance of

doing a good job,

and striving for excellence.

Lost

One moment I am completely at home

comfortable

in my element and in my skin.

Then

something happens and I'm lost—

no longer among friends

no longer able to trust

let alone feel comfort.

I withdraw into my shell,

and am leery of anyone coming near.

Perpetuating hate

"Mostly they are worried about the daughters—

and rightly so!"

I only nod, afraid that words would

betray my anger.

I know what he means—

he has already told me that she has

"become a lesbian—she's gone crazy!"

They think of lesbians as deviants—

people with no redeeming value—

tainting all they touch.

I want to scream

I want to tell him

that the only ones

who are likely to harm the children

are closed minded people like him.

People who will teach them to hate

anyone who is different.

Secrets

Sometimes because I want to

and sometimes because others

choose to ignore—

I fade away.

But I'm watchful, always aware

of other's actions and of the

stolen glances.

I can tell you your innermost thoughts,

dreams,

yearnings.

I know things that you don't

even know about yourself.

Phoenix

I share your pain and feel your joys

from afar.

I peer into your world.

I applaud you silently,

as do I shed the tears.

I mentally calculate your accomplishments

and note your failures,

knowing that you will find a way—

the best way to grow from them.

I've known you through your highs

and the lowest of lows.

I have seen you rise like a phoenix

from the ashes.

Codependence

I am not a keeper of your emotions.

For years I've done everything

to make sure that you are okay

and possibly happy too.

There have been times

that I've forgotten to make sure

of my own well-being.

So from here on out,

the responsibility shifts back to you.

Mother's Day

You don't feel what I feel

so don't even pretend.

I am a mother

without her children.

And a child

without a mother.

What does that make me?

erased?

insignificant?

Mother's Day is hardest of all.

I just can't seem to escape it.

Everywhere you turn,

people are talking about Mother's Day.

I trudge through, with my head down,

hoping to not be noticed.

Hoping to not be engaged in a conversation

or wished a Happy Mother's Day.

Shame

I see the blanket draped across her couch.

Memories flood over me.

I see in my minds eye the blanket on my bed,

protecting me from cold,

wrapped around my babies

filling them with warmth.

I had pledged for years to make Christmas stockings

from this very blanket,

to preserve memories and create new ones

and now,

the very fact that it is draped across her couch

fills me with shame.

All of my best intentions have been left undone.

All of my goals put on the back burner.

This blanket symbolizes

every ounce of my shame.

Assimilating

I think of all of the forgotten passions...

I think back to all of the things that I've enjoyed

in life.

I wonder how to weave them all together

to create the perfect life—

the perfect me.

Paul the Seaside Treasure

We wandered into a hidden bookstore,

looking for treasure.

We looked at the books,

saw nothing too noteworthy,

meandered through,

then, as we were about to leave,

he spoke to me.

I had noticed him,

sitting by himself,

with a crude set of watercolors.

He mumbled and he stammered,

he had no social grace.

Then he presented me

with a piece of his soul.

He painted us three paintings,

each one more amazing than the last.

The Dance

It's all a dance.

Intimacy.

Anger. Fear.

Love. Loss.

Seduction.

Betrayal.

At times the dance is exhilarating

other times, it's exhausting.

As with any dance, though

you move in circles, large and small...

always destined to repeat the same moves.

If you are lucky—

and willing to continue,

your skill will increase

and the dance becomes easier,

more pleasing,

more fulfilling.

Memories

There are times when I wax nostalgic

and I miss you.

Then I remember how it felt to be around you.

Being a witness to your hypocrisy was maddening.

Feeling angry and manipulated.

Anger and manipulation

spoonfed to me regularly,

sprinkle with a pinch of guilt.

I tried to gag it down,

fighting the urge to vomit.

There were good times,

don't think I've forgotten.

However, the bad far outweighs

the good.

Home Again

They say you can never go home again.

I wholeheartedly agree.

If you live in the present—

pursue all that is good

towards inner peace

Then home comes to you.

Love will come

happiness will come

home, and life,

will come to you.

The Battle

I know all of the reasons why not

and none of the reasons why.

I know all of the things I can

warn myself against

and listen not to the treaties of others.

There is a battle going on

and none of it can be seen.

I can feel the searing wounds and no one

knows the pain that I alone feel.

No one cares, no one else dies—

everyone around me moves forward,

marching as one.

Recharge

I just don't feel like being "the good wife" today

I can't fill those shoes.

And for once, I don't even want to try.

Nope,

no failures for me today.

No unsuccessful attempts.

Am I being utterly selfish?

Some would say yes.

But I would like to un-label "selfish"

and re-label simply "recharging".

Solitude

I find that my time of most

personal growth is during solitude.

Don't misunderstand—I need people

but I need them when I need them.

When I am alone,

I have the chance to branch out and grow.

I stake claim at any free moments

and guard them as a mother would her young.

If this time is interrupted—or denied me,

my frustration flows into other areas of my life

Empath

I have become

a noticer

of things not spoken

of looks not given

of feelings never revealed.

I am an empath,

clairvoyant,

observant...

depending on your views.

Regardless, I know the things

never expressed.

It is a gift,

wrapped in a burden

knowing how other's feel

even about you.

But along with knowing, I also understand.

Lessons

I think of the children—

three amazing boys.

I wish I could sit them down

and tell them how to live:

be true to yourself

always do the right thing.

I wish I could build a dam against any pain

that might come their way.

But I know better.

I know that everything happens for a reason

Sometimes pain is the catalyst needed for growth.

I know that any pain they feel we will also feel,

that can't be helped.

We will continue to feel pride at their growth

we will hold them when they stumble,

worry when they are faced with difficult times.

And always we will teach them.

Teach them to own up to their mistakes,

and to right their wrongs.

We will show them how to find the good in others,

and support them when they realize

that sometimes the best thing is to

give someone space.

We will continue to show them how to love,

because we know that even when no words are spoken—

perhaps especially then—

they see and they learn.

Tossed Away

What the world saw in our story was an ending

I saw it as a continuation, a changed reality,

but not an end.

Love morphed into friendship

and I offered encouragement as able,

when asked.

Always lending a shoulder and an unbiased response

I can take the love ending

But your ultimate betrayal

was when you threw the friendship away.

The Journey

I am so proud

to see the man that you've become

You have forged your own path

and not bent to other's will

No matter how hard they pushed

I wish I could snap my fingers

and make your dreams come true

but you know as well as I

that the journey is half the fun

Still Here

I know your innermost secrets,

all the things you have been afraid

to share with anyone before.

I think the telling of them has been a test

every time

to see if I would run away

or even look at you differently.

But I am still here.

I know your heart

and I am not going anywhere.

Adios

I seem to have once again

overstayed my usefulness.

I always want to save the day

and be helpful

but then I linger,

paralyzed

afraid of yet more change

and I stay

long past the time that it serves me

to be here.

No More

I don't know why you chose me

to be a keeper of your secrets

but I don't consent to that.

Your lies do not buy my loyalty

and your promises

don't make me silent.

My attempts at an authentic life

are thwarted by your dishonesty

and I no longer accept it.

Your Highness

You act entitled

sitting on your throne

ordering others around,

not pulling your own weight,

not contributing.

Do you really think all of those

you think of as 'minions'

will have your back?

How long do you think

they will willingly take orders?

The uprising is soon,

and you will have none

on your side.

Obligations

Things I have to do

seem to always over-rule

things I want to do.

Laundry needs to be done,

dishes need to be washed,

bathrooms need to be scrubbed.

Yet, poetry yearns to be written,

letters beg to be mailed,

paintings whisper that they

are ready to be born.

Yet, I launder, scrub, and wash

and the want to's get

moved to the back burner

Time Marches

There was a time that we were inseparable

not a day went by that we didn't spend time together

our love was unique and life-altering

and then life happened

and we drifted apart.

Years later, close to a decade,

you found me again

and it is a bittersweet reunion.

You have your love,

I have mine

and where do we fit?

Love

I love you in a way

that I have never loved before.

This love brightens

the colors I see,

enhances the flavors in all I eat,

Makes the silences magical,

and the words truly inspired.

Breaking Family Ties

You can pick your friends

but you can't pick your family.

That's what they say.

I've always said "I have to love you,

but I don't have to like you"

However, you've tested my

theory.

Do I have to love you?

I haven't liked you for years

I have tried,

so many times.

But war has been waged

and the price of war may just be

that we can never go back again.

Crawl Inside You

You intrigue me

do you even realize that?

I am completely enamoured

and would love to crawl inside your skin

and be you,

see things through your eyes,

feel what you feel.

I would love to hear the inner monologue

and be able to understand

all of your gestures and comments.

I would love to crawl right inside you

and know every inch.

Acceptance

I no longer

make apologies

for who I am.

I spent years doing just that

out loud,

and in my own head.

For years I chastised myself

for not fitting in

for being weird

for saying the wrong thing

for saying nothing at all.

But I no longer make apologies

I realize that I am exactly

who I am

and where I am

supposed to be.

At Last

We were so late to the game

late in finding one another

late in finding a common ground.

But once we did,

we dove in,

we didn't dip our toes in the water,

or test it, awkwardly,

we dove in and never looked back.

I am so thankful for our love.

So thankful for the time that I had you.

Thankful for all the memories

and lessons

and trials

and tears.

You taught me so much

in both life

and in death.

What a Ride

In my life

I have laughed til I cried

and cried til I puked.

I have sobbed silently

and wailed loudly.

I have had moments torn between

crying from loss

and laughing from a memory.

What a ride it has been

What a ride it has been.

In my life

I have loved

and I have left

and I have chosen to not look back.

What a ride it has been.

3 A CONCLUSION

This chapter should be called "A conclusion of sorts". It is indeed a conclusion of this compilation. However, I am more certain than ever that there will be many more poems to come through me. Poetry has been a constant in my life.

I was in high school when *"Dead Poet's Society"* came out. I will never forget going to the cave with Gretel, Zach, and so many others to read poetry by flashlight. We would hike down, one by one, each carrying a flashlight and a book of poetry. We would munch on chocolate covered espresso beans and read poetry out loud to one another. It was my idea of heaven.

Poetry yearns to be spoken aloud, to be shared, to be savored. In fact, I will go so far as to say that if more people would take a moment and appreciate poetry each day, the world would be a much more peaceful place.

If you would like to share some poetry with me privately or have me share it on my blog, please email me at robynlinz@gmail.com . Use that same email if you would simply like to comment on one of my poems. My dream is that I stirred a little something within you. Perhaps I made you smile, or laugh, or think perhaps you are not the only one. If so, my job is done.

Thank you so much for being here. I bow to you, dear reader. You are the reason I write, and the reason that I will continue.

www.ingramcontent.com/pod-product-compliance
Lightning Source LLC
Chambersburg PA
CBHW071641040426
42452CB00009B/1719